CONTENTS

A minimalist no bullshit guide to Faith, God and the Good Life

LIVING ON EARTH

DEDICATION

To the Universe

ACKNOWLEDGMENTS

Thanks to all people that have lived before me.

1 CHAPTER ONE

Believe.

[This page is intentionally left blank]

[This page is intentionally left blank]

[This page is intentionally left blank]

[This page is intentionally left blank]

[This page is intentionally left blank]

[This page is intentionally left blank]

[This page is intentionally left blank]

[This page is intentionally left blank]

[This page is intentionally left blank]

[This page is intentionally left blank]

[This page is intentionally left blank]

[This page is intentionally left blank]

[This page is intentionally left blank]

[This page is intentionally left blank]

[This page is intentionally left blank]

[This page is intentionally left blank]

[This page is intentionally left blank]

[This page is intentionally left blank]

[This page is intentionally left blank]

[This page is intentionally left blank]

[This page is intentionally left blank]

ABOUT THE AUTHOR

Living on Earth – the author of the "A minimalist no bullshit guide" series.

Printed in Great Britain
by Amazon